Dear Parents:

Congratulations! Your child is taking the first steps on an exciting journey. The destination? Independent reading!

STEP INTO READING® will help your child get there. The program offers five steps to reading success. Each step includes fun stories and colorful art or photographs. In addition to original fiction and books with favorite characters, there are Step into Reading Non-Fiction Readers, Phonics Readers and Boxed Sets, Sticker Readers, and Comic Readers—a complete literacy program with something to interest every child.

Learning to Read, Step by Step!

Ready to Read   Preschool–Kindergarten
• big type and easy words • rhyme and rhythm • picture clues
For children who know the alphabet and are eager to begin reading.

Reading with Help   Preschool–Grade 1
• basic vocabulary • short sentences • simple stories
For children who recognize familiar words and sound out new words with help.

Reading on Your Own   Grades 1–3
• engaging characters • easy-to-follow plots • popular topics
For children who are ready to read on their own.

Reading Paragraphs   Grades 2–3
• challenging vocabulary • short paragraphs • exciting stories
For newly independent readers who read simple sentences with confidence.

Ready for Chapters   Grades 2–4
• chapters • longer paragraphs • full-color art
For children who want to take the plunge into chapter books but still like colorful pictures.

STEP INTO READING® is designed to give every child a successful reading experience. The grade levels are only guides; children will progress through the steps at their own speed, developing confidence in their reading. The F&P Text Level on the back cover serves as another tool to help you choose the right book for your child.

Remember, a lifetime love of reading starts with a single step!

To Magali Messac,
the ballerina on the cover of the magazine

All rights reserved. Published in the United States by
Random House Children's Books, a division of Random House LLC,
a Penguin Random House Company, New York.

Step into Reading, Random House, and the Random House colophon are
registered trademarks of Random House LLC.

Visit us on the Web!
StepIntoReading.com
randomhouse.com/kids

Educators and librarians, for a variety of teaching tools,
visit us at RHTeachersLibrarians.com

Library of Congress Cataloging-in-Publication Data is available upon request.
ISBN 978-0-385-75515-3 (trade) – ISBN 978-0-385-75516-0 (lib. bdg.) –
ISBN 978-0-385-75517-7 (ebook)

Printed in the United States of America 10 9 8 7 6 5 4 3 2 1

This book has been officially leveled by using the F&P Text Level Gradient™ Leveling System.

PHOTO CREDITS

American Broadcasting Companies, Inc./Peter "Hopper" Stone: 37

DePrince family: 3, 6, 8, 9, 17, 18, 21, 22, 23, 39, 44, 47, 48 (top right), 48 (bottom right)

Johannesburg Ballet: 48 (bottom left)

Bess Kargman: 35, 36

Matthew Murphy and Dance Theatre of Harlem: 48 (top left)

Rachel Neville and Dance Theatre of Harlem: 43

Ballerina Dreams

From Orphan to Dancer

by Michaela DePrince and Elaine DePrince
illustrated by Frank Morrison

Random House 🏠 New York

1

The Ballerina

It is a chilly night in December. I stand backstage wearing leg warmers and a sweatshirt, but I'm still shivering.

"Five minutes, Michaela!" I hear. It's time for me to dance. I stretch my legs and point my toes to get them ready.

I check my tiara to make sure it's not loose, and fluff out my pink tutu.

The knots in my pointe shoe ribbons are tied nice and tight. I wouldn't want them to slip off during the performance.

I peek through the stage curtains and see the eager faces of the audience. They are waiting for the ballerina to appear.

The music begins, and my heart beats fast with excitement. I fly onto the stage. *I am the ballerina!*

2

The Orphan Girl

Long before I became a ballerina, I was an orphan in Sierra Leone, a country in western Africa. My parents died there in the ongoing war. I was sent to an orphanage (*OR-fuh-nidge*), where children without parents live.

There were twenty-seven children in the orphanage, but I was the only one with a condition called vitiligo (*vih-tuh-LIE-go*). The vitiligo made some of my skin lose its color. I have white spots on my brown skin.

Some of the other children laughed at my spots. They called me names, and I often felt sad.

One girl never laughed at me. Her name was Mia, and she became my best

friend. We shared a grass mat to sleep on at bedtime. We shared our rice at mealtime. Mia sang to me and told me stories. I taught Mia how to play new games.

Sometimes I would miss my parents very much, but I would not cry in front of the other children. Instead, I would sit at the orphanage gate alone and let my tears flow.

One windy day, a magazine blew down the road in front of the gate. I reached out and caught it.

A pretty picture of a woman was on the front cover of the magazine. She wore a short pink dress that stuck out around her in a circle. She had pink shoes on her feet and stood on the tips of her toes. She looked very happy.

"I want to be happy and beautiful

like you someday!" I said to the woman in the picture as I wiped away my tears.

I showed the picture to Mia and then I folded it and hid it in my clothes. I didn't want anybody to take it away from me.

The next day, I showed my teacher the picture.

"Who is this woman? What is she doing? Why is she wearing these strange pink clothes?" I asked Teacher Sarah.

"This woman is a famous ballerina. She is wearing a tutu and pointe shoes because she is dancing ballet," Teacher Sarah explained.

"Do you think that I can be a ballerina like her someday?" I asked.

"You can become a ballerina, too, if you take lessons for many years, if you work hard, and if you practice every day."

Whoa! So many ifs! "If I can take lessons, I will work hard. I will practice every day!" I exclaimed. "I want to become a ballerina."

3

Getting Adopted

One night, Papa Andrew, the director of the orphanage, told all of us, "It is time to leave Sierra Leone. We must go to a country where there is no war. There you will meet the families who will adopt you and take you to live in America."

We traveled on foot with Papa Andrew, walking over the mountains and through the jungle. At night, the sounds of the jungle terrified us. We slept close together, trembling with fear. Mia sang to me to help me feel better, and I played hand-clapping games with her.

Finally we reached safety, and Papa

Andrew took us to meet our new mothers
and fathers.

I held Mia's hand. My knees began to
shake and my heart began to pound. What
if I never saw Mia again? I worried that
my new parents wouldn't like my spots.
I worried that they would not let me dance
ballet.

A woman with hair the color of daisies

opened her arms and hugged Mia. I was
happy that Mia had a new mother but
felt sad that we wouldn't live together
anymore. But then the lady pulled me into
her arms, too! Mia and I were going to live
together. This woman was our new mama.

My best friend and I would be sisters!
Then I did cry. I cried tears of joy.

Our new mama had a lot of presents for
my sister and me. Mia loved the sneakers
with lights on the bottom. I searched through
my mother's bags, but I could not find pink
shoes for dancing ballet.

My mother wanted to know what I
was looking for. I could not remember the

4

My New Life

In America, we had food, warm clothes, and lots of love. Mia and I went to many fun places with our parents and our new brothers.

One day, Mama took us to a store. There I found a video with ballerinas on the box.

the Sugar Plum Fairy. I dreamed of the day I would dance onstage in the real *Nutcracker.*

Soon I would know enough English to take ballet lessons!

5

Ballet Lessons

"Wake up, Michaela! Wake up, Mia! Today is the day of your first ballet lesson," Mama called one Saturday morning.

My eyes popped open and I leaped out of bed.

In ballet class, our teacher explained to the students that all ballet words are French. She said, "That is because the first professional (*pruh-FEH-shuh-nul*) ballet company, the Paris Opera Ballet, was started in France, more than three hundred and fifty years ago."

At the beginning of every class, we lined up and held the barre (*bar*). Next, we learned how to stand in the five positions of ballet. Then we practiced how to hold our arms. "This is called port de bras (*por duh BRA*), which means 'position of the arms,'" our teacher explained.

The teacher showed us how to tendu (*tahn-DOO*), which means "stretched" in French. I watched her carefully.

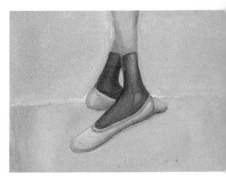

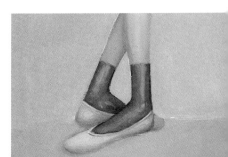

When she stood in fifth position, I did, too.

"Stretch out your leg and point your toes," she said as we put out our right legs. Next, she stepped onto her right foot. I did, too.

I looked down in surprise. I had tendued from fifth position to second position!

Now our teacher said, "Bend your knees a little. And straighten them again. Good. You just did a plié (*plee-AY*)."
I learned that plié means "bent" in French.

Putting ballet steps together is called a combination (*com-buh-NAY-shun*). That day, I did my first ballet combination! I felt so proud!

During one class, my ballet teacher put her sweatshirt in the middle of the floor. Then she leaped over it. "That is a grand jeté (*grahn zhuh-TAY*)," she said. "Now *you* will try it."

When I leaped across the floor, I felt like I was flying. I loved that feeling. The grand jeté became my favorite step.

I learned more steps with each lesson. I did a leap that made me look like a cat with hot feet. I laughed when I learned that it was called pas de chat (*pah duh SHAH*), or "cat step."

Every day, I practiced new steps and combinations. When I was seven and a half years old, my teacher decided that I was ready to dance on my toes. This is called dancing en pointe (*on point*).

I needed to buy special shoes to dance en pointe. My new pointe shoes were silky soft and beautiful. When I put them on my feet, I looked like the ballerina on the cover of the magazine.

Now I practiced harder than before. Soon I was dancing en pointe on the stage.

6

My First Nutcracker

When I was eight years old, I auditioned for *The Nutcracker.*

I looked for black children in the party scene of the video that I owned, but I didn't see any. I worried that I would not get chosen for *The Nutcracker.*

When I went to the audition, I danced my very best. I hoped that I would be cast as a party girl or a polichinelle (*pah-lee-shuh-NELL*), one of the little children who dance out from under Mother Ginger's dress.

At the end of the audition, the *Nutcracker* director gave each of us an

envelope. "Do not open this until you get downstairs!" he warned. My knees shook all the way down the steps. Finally I reached the first floor and opened the envelope. When I saw the words "party girl" and "polichinelle girl," I thought I would faint!

That year, I had a thrilling time dancing in *The Nutcracker.* Best of all, I decided that if I could be a black party girl and a black polichinelle girl, then someday I could surely be a black Sugar Plum Fairy.

7

In Front of a Camera

One day, I got a phone call from a movie producer named Bess Kargman, who wanted to make a movie about ballet. "It's a documentary," Bess explained. "I would like you to be in it, Michaela."

I was shy, so at first I said, "No, thank you."

Mama said, "Bess's film will give you a chance to show the world that black girls *can* be ballerinas."

There are few professional black ballerinas. Many people have never seen a black ballerina. So I thought about what Mama said. Then I changed my mind.

6 dancers
5 minutes on stage
1 chance to make it

FIRST POSITION

A film by BESS KARGMAN

"Yes," I told Bess. "I would like to be in your film."

Bess and her film crew followed me around with cameras. They filmed me practicing ballet and dancing in a big

competition in New York City called the
Youth America Grand Prix (*grahn pree*).

During the competition, I injured my
left ankle. It felt hot and swollen, and I
wasn't sure if I would be able to dance.

I decided to continue anyway and ended up winning a scholarship to the famous Jacqueline Kennedy Onassis School of the American Ballet Theatre in New York City.

People all over the world saw Bess's movie, which is called *First Position*. And it won many important awards.

Some people who saw the film wanted to know more about me. They invited me to be on television programs and featured

me in magazines. They asked me questions about being a black ballerina.

I was still shy, so sometimes it was hard for me to answer the questions. Then I would remember the many messages that kids everywhere sent me after they saw *First Position.*

One girl wrote, "You are my hero." Another wrote, "I want to grow up to dance like you." Messages like these made me feel brave. Maybe I could inspire other kids to study ballet, just as the woman in the magazine picture had inspired me.

8

A Dream Come True

My dream has come true. I am now a real ballerina, a professional dancer. That means I dance for a living. My favorite step is still the grand jeté. Many people call me the ballerina who flies.

I have been lucky to dance wonderful roles in many different ballets. I have even danced the role of the Sugar Plum Fairy in *The Nutcracker.*

My dancing has taken me to many countries. Sometimes I dance on grand stages; other times I dance in small auditoriums. Once I even performed in a barn. I have danced for rich people and poor people, for all ages and races.

Dancing brings me great joy. I love knowing that my dancing also brings joy to others.

I have learned not to be shy. When I travel, I enjoy talking to people, especially children. Many kids ask me, "How can I make my dream come true?"

I tell them, "It doesn't matter if you dream of being a doctor, a teacher, a writer, *or* a ballerina. Every dream begins with one step. After that, you must work hard and practice every day. If you never give up, your dream *will* come true."

About the Authors

Michaela DePrince studied on scholarship at the Rock School for Dance Education and the Jacqueline Kennedy Onassis School at the American Ballet Theatre. Michaela is now a professional ballerina. She was named the youngest principal dancer for the Dance Theatre of Harlem and is dancing with the Dutch National Ballet, one of the top classical ballet companies in the world.

Michaela starred in the ballet documentary *First Position,* which was nominated for an NAACP Image Award. She has also appeared on *Dancing with the Stars,* as well as *Good Morning America, Nightline, BBC News,* and other news programs in the United States and internationally. In 2012, the *Huffington Post* named her one of their 18 Under 18: *HuffPost Teen*'s List of the Most Amazing People of the Year. You can visit her online at michaeladeprince.com or on Twitter at @michdeprince.

Elaine DePrince is Michaela's adoptive mother and co-author. She is the author of *Cry Bloody Murder: A Tale of Tainted Blood,* as well as a songwriter and owner of Sweet Mocha Music LLC, an Indie record label and music publishing business. A graduate of Rutgers University and a former special education teacher, Elaine, after raising five sons, took a leave of absence from law school in 1999 to adopt a child from war-torn West Africa. She often says that the need was so great that she ended up with six West African daughters.

Elaine lives in New York City with her husband and their five youngest daughters.